NO LONGER
ANYTHIN
RANGEVIEW L

D0624857

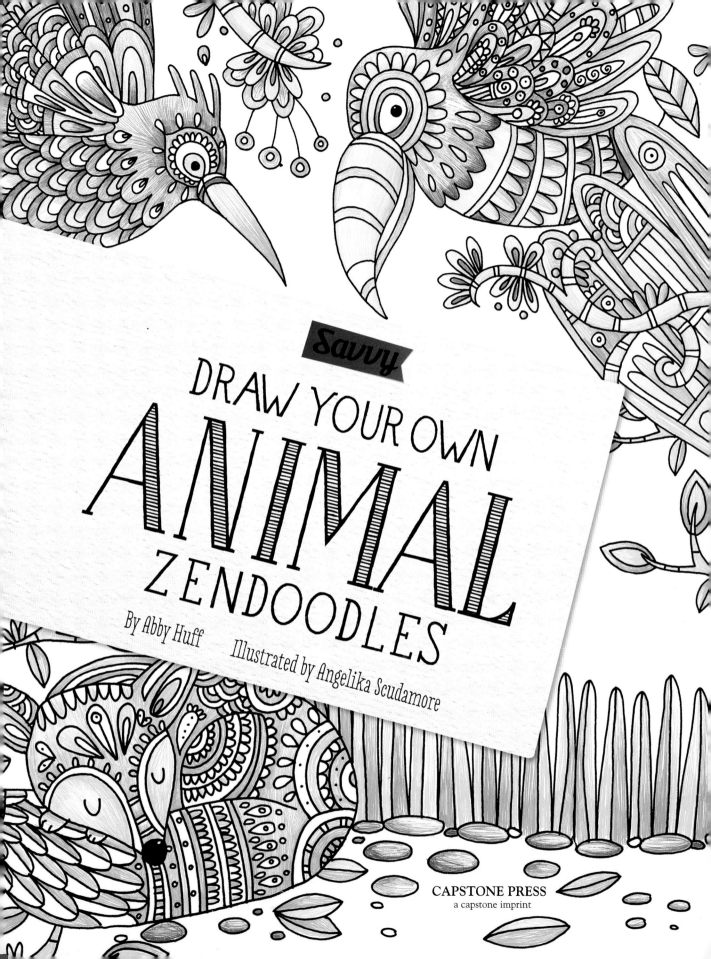

DRAW YOUR OWN ANIMAL ZENDOODLES

Savvy

By Abby Huff

Illustrated by Angelika Scudamore

CAPSTONE PRESS
a capstone imprint

Savvy Books are published by Capstone Press, a Capstone imprint
1710 Roe Crest Drive
North Mankato, Minnesota 56003
www.mycapstone.com

Copyright © 2017 by Capstone. All rights reserved. No part of this publication may be reproduced in whole or in part, or stored in a retrieval system, or transmitted in any form or by any means, electronic, mechanical, photocopying, recording, or otherwise, without written permission of the publisher.

Library of Congress Cataloging-in-Publication Data
Names: Huff, Abby, 1991– author. | Scudamore, Angelika, illustrator.
Title: Draw your own animal zendoodles / by Abby Huff ; illustrated by
   Angelika Scudamore.
Description: North Mankato, Minnesota : Capstone, 2017. | Series: Savvy.
   Draw your own zendoodles | Audience: Ages 9–13. | Audience: Grades 4 to 8.
Identifiers: LCCN 2016044394 | ISBN 9781515748403 (library binding) |
   ISBN 9781515748472 (ebook pdf)
Subjects: LCSH: Animals in art—Juvenile literature. | Drawing—Technique—
   Juvenile literature. | Handicraft for children—Juvenile literature.
Classification: LCC NC780 .H74 2017 | DDC 743.6—dc23
LC record available at https://lccn.loc.gov/2016044394

Editorial Credits
Bobbie Nuytten, designer; Jo Miller, media researcher; Laura Manthe, premedia specialist

Image Credits
Capstone Studio: Karon Dubke, 7 (all), 21, 44-47 (all), Shutterstock: Danyskar, 38 (gemstones), 39 (gemstone), DragoNika, 17, gresei, 15, ILeysen, 38 (diamond shapes), robert_s, 40, saraporn, 10, swoon, 25 (watercolor waves), Zadorozhnyi Viktor, 34 (paintbrush); Backgrounds: Shutterstock: aopsan, arigato, CCat82, donatas1205, happykanppy, Lana Veshta, macknimal, Mikhail Pogosov, Nik Merkulov, Only background, Piotr Zajc, Ratana21, redstone, siriak kaewgorn, Turbojet, Vadim Georgiev

Crafts created by Lori Blackwell and Tyson J. Schultz

Printed and bound in the United States of America.
010062S17

Table of Contents

Zendoodle Basics

Ever feel stressed? Unwind with zendoodles! These elegant designs are built up from easy patterns and are perfect for relaxing. Don't worry about creating flawless drawings. Instead, focus on one stroke at time. Tap into your creative side, and when in doubt, do whatever feels right. You'll soon get wild with animal zendoodles, but first start simple with a few fundamentals. Dive into the world of inspiring zendoodles!

Patterns

Zendoodles may look complicated, but they're created from basic patterns. Make patterns by repeating and layering different strokes and shapes. Using multiple designs in a zendoodle gives it its signature tangled style.

Shapes and Motifs

Small shapes and motifs (a fancy word for recurring forms and elements) can be used to help fill a zendoodle. Use teardrops, fans, circles, flowers, and more. Try drawing a cluster of shapes in your zendoodle or spread them out. Decorate them with dots, lines, or a pattern for an elaborate look.

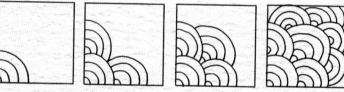

Adding Patterns

Adding patterns is the most fun and calming part of
the zendoodle process. There are two main methods.
Try both to see which you like best.

Sectioned
Divide your drawing with lines.
Fill each section with a pattern.

Free-formed
Let your patterns overlap and run
into each other. When you're done,
it should be hard to tell where one
pattern begins and another ends.

Object Zendoodles

Zendoodles don't have to resemble anything. You can simply fill a page with intricate designs. Other times, it's fun to make your zendoodle into a recognizable object, like a cat or jellyfish. When you're working with an object, try experimenting with these two methods.

Positive space
Draw inside the object. This is using the positive space — the space occupied by a subject. Decorate within the lines using adorable details and doodles.

Negative space
Draw around the object. This is using the negative space — the space around a subject. For maximum impact, don't add any details inside the object. Leave it completely blank for a striking graphic look.

Warm Up
Loosen your wrist and relax your mind. Get started with zigzags, squiggles, dots, curls, and more.

Zendoodle Tools & Materials

If you have a pencil and a scrap of paper, you're ready to zendoodle! But it can be fun to try out supplies too. Here are a few essentials to keep in your toolbox.

Pencils

The most basic doodle tool. Try a mechanical pencil for consistently precise, even lines.

Paper

A page from your notebook can do in a pinch. For best results, use drawing or sketch paper. The thicker paper will hold up better to erasing and marking. Paper also comes in different textures. Generally, it'll be easier to doodle on a smooth surface.

Pens

Pens are perfect for polished zendoodles. Splurge on drawing pens for smoother, high quality lines. Look for archival or pigment ink pens. The special ink won't smudge or fade, so it'll keep your design looking pretty.

Colors

Zendoodles are bold in black and white, but color adds a whole new dimension. Use colored pencils for a soft look. Try markers and colored pens for dramatic color. There are many options to choose from. Enjoy experimenting!

Quick and Easy Zendoodles

Not feeling confident in your drawing abilities? Want to start doodling right away? Head to **capstonekids.com**. There you can download sheets with blank outlines. Simply print the page and you're ready to go. Add exciting patterns and designs to make it your own.

Cuddly Hedgehog

No need to worry about pokey spines here! This little zendoodle hedgehog is ready to snuggle up. Get started with teardrop shapes shown below. Or design your own angular pattern for a pricklier look.

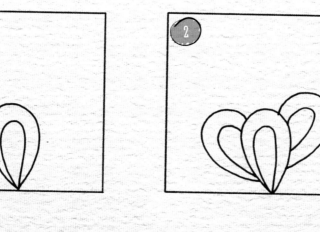

Dreamy Jellyfish

Get swept up in a gentle ocean current with these jellyfish. Draw tentacles that drift across the page. The wavy lines will create the illusion of floating in water. Delicate charms along your jellyfish's tentacles add to the whimsical feel.

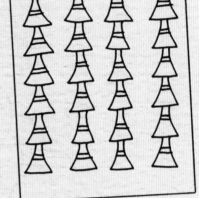

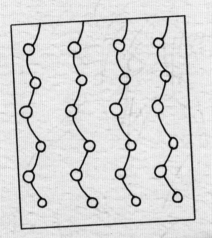

Charmed

Build vertical doodles out of little charms for a cute look. Try spacing them out or using a mix of doodles in one line. Experiment with the charms below or create ones that reflect your personality and interests.

Pretty Kitty

Curving shapes and laid-back details mix to make an elegant cat. To fill your feline, focus on drawing a few large forms. Divide them up into layers. Add little patterns and embellishments to each section to complete the zendoodle.

Kaleidoscope Turtles

These turtles are ready for some pizzazz! Draw hexagons inside the shell and then start doodling. Decorate the shapes with a repeating motif or a beautiful flower. For a creative challenge, come up with a new design for each hexagon.

Color It!

Turn your zendoodles into custom coloring pages. If you drew in pencil, trace over your design with black pen. A waterproof or archival quality pen is best. The ink won't bleed if you color over it. Now you're ready to start coloring with your favorite tool. Or, before you color, make photocopies of your zendoodle. That way you can color it again and again. You could even host a coloring party for you and your friends!

Fantastic Fox

Give this clever animal some quirky cuteness. Add rows of simple patterns and twirly doodles. Try leaving a few areas blank for more visual interest. Skip drawing on parts of the face, chest, and tail to recreate the fox's white fur.

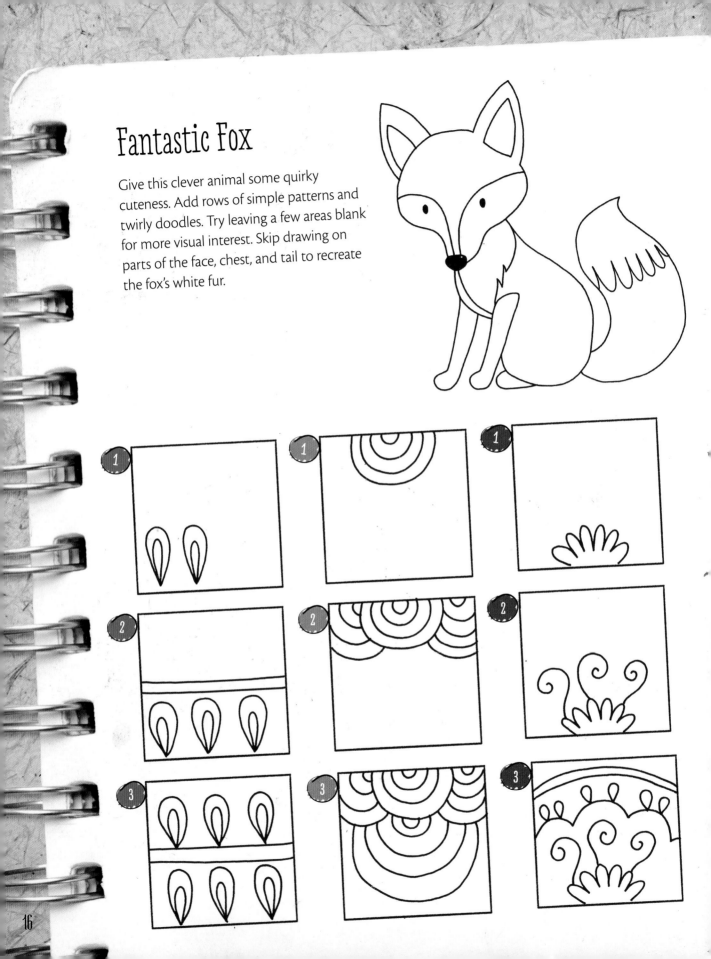

Awesome Owls

Ready to ruffle some feathers? Give these wise birds a unique style. Use layered teardrop shapes for the feathers on the wings. Draw long, thin petals to fill the body. Decorate the plumage with playful patterns and you're sure to have a hoot!

19

Charming Fish

There may be hundreds of fish in the sea, but this zendoodle fish is one of a kind. Draw the fins extra big. That'll give you plenty of space to create exotic patterns on your fish's scales.

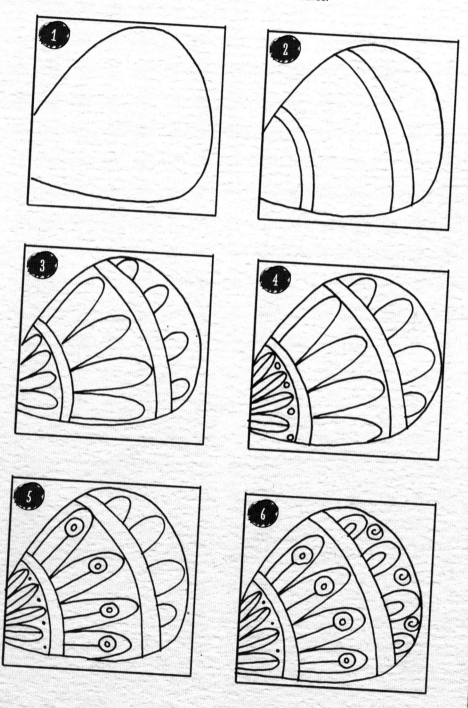

Creative Colored Pens

Freshen up your zendoodles and draw with colored pens! Switch out your black pen for bright neons, cool pastels, or sparkly glitter gel inks.

Here are a few ways to use your colored pens:

- Use one colored pen for the whole zendoodle.
- Pick a couple of colors. Doodle a large section in one color. Draw the next section in a new color. Alternate throughout the zendoodle.
- Draw the large shapes in your zendoodle using one color. Use other colors to make the patterns.
- Doodle in pen. Then take out colored pencils and color in your design. Choose hues similar to the pen for a coordinated look.

Prancing Pony

This horse is ready to parade its lovely looks. To create a free-flowing tail and mane, use a mix of lines. Draw thick ones filled with small patterns and add skinny strokes adorned with whirly circles. For the body, focus on making a few larger shapes. Decorate them with show-worthy designs.

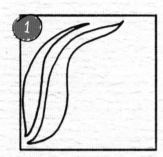

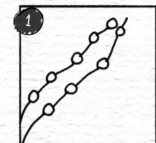

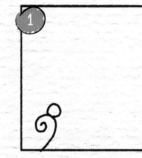

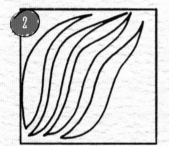

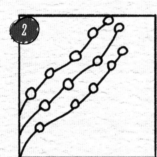

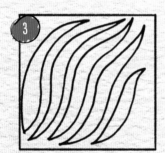

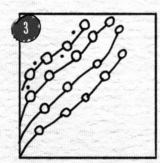

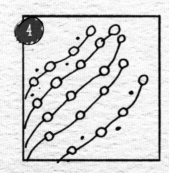

Jumping Dolphin

Make a splash! Divide your dolphin drawing into sections. Mark off the face, the belly, the fins, the flippers, the midsection, and the tail. Sprinkle a new doodle in each section. The swirly pattern below is a perfect way to capture the feel of rolling waves.

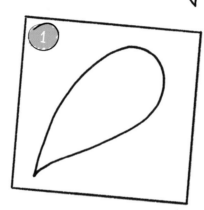

Top Dog

This pup is ready to be leader of the pack with his perky attitude. Mix lots of patterns for a bold look. You can even be inspired by dog toys for your design. Can you create a doodle based on a doggie bone? Try it out!

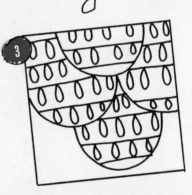

1 **2** **3**

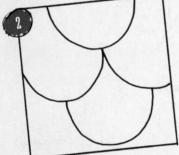

1 **2** **3**

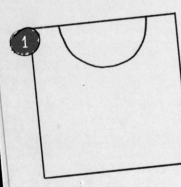

1 **2** **3**

1 **2** **3**

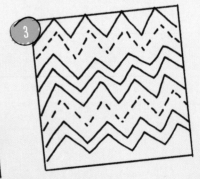

27

Magical Sea Horses

Create an underwater fantasy! Add floral details to these dainty fish. Start with petals fanning out from the belly. Try rounded, pointed, or triangular shapes. Be inspired by the finished examples to design the rest of your sea horse.

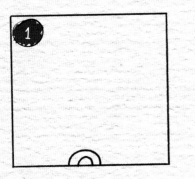 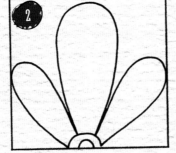 

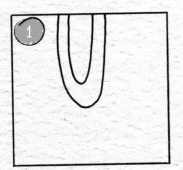 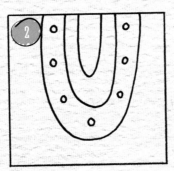 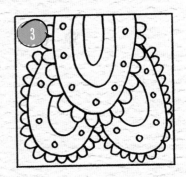

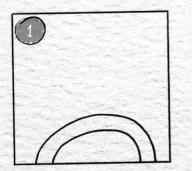  

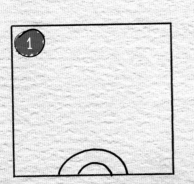 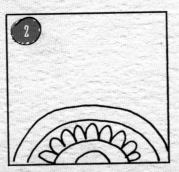 

29

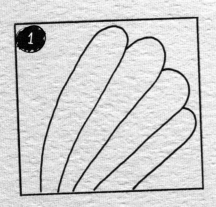

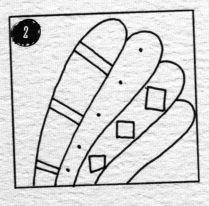

Tropical Hummingbird

Real birds zip by in a flash, but your zendoodle hummingbird will sit pretty for all to see! Recreate their endless energy. Pack each feather with intricate doodles. Mix diagonal and vertical lines for a simple pattern that hums with excitement.

Wild Stripes Zebra

Your zebra will be styling with its special stripes. Use the patterns below to start out, but don't be afraid to get creative. Embellish the lines with diamonds, checkers, dots, or whatever feels right. If you want to make the zebra's short hair equally fabulous, look back at page 23 for magnificent mane motifs!

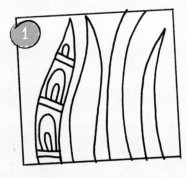 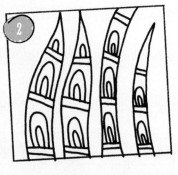

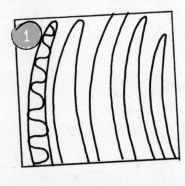 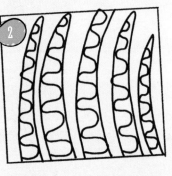

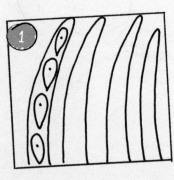 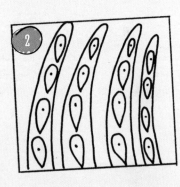

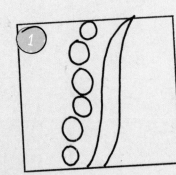 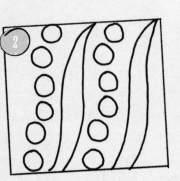 

Majestic Lion

Make a mane fit for a king. Start around the head. Then layer curls and feathery shapes. Go wild and see if you can fill a whole page with a maze of tangled doodles. Add a tropical flower or two in the mane for a jungle vibe.

Adding Watercolor

For a soft splash of color, try watercolors. Start with thick drawing or watercolor paper. With a large brush, apply a thin layer of water to the page. Load your brush with watercolor and paint onto the wet paper. Create the general shape of your design or try an abstract form. Dry completely before doodling over it with pencil or pen.

Proud Peacock

These fancy birds are known for their impressive feathers and distinctive eyespots. Decorate your zendoodle peacock with any type of feather you can imagine. Try a mix of feather shapes. Go long and short, wide and thin, or pointed and rounded. Let them swoop across the page in a regal display.

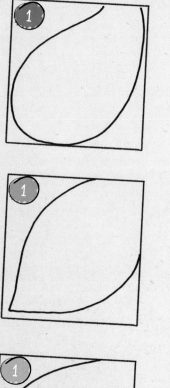
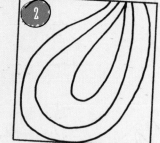
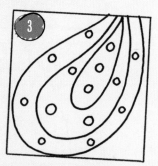

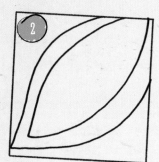
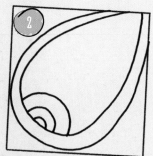
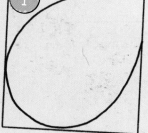

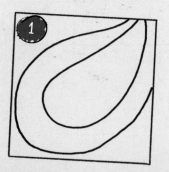
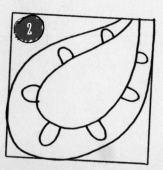

Glittering Gems

Bring sophistication to your zendoodles with gems. Sketch one and make it gleam with color. Study pictures to see how color changes across a jewel. Or, try coloring a gradient. Go from dark to light. Use a white gel pen to add spots of shine along the edge. It'll help create a three-dimensional look.

For a quick and hassle-free approach, use stick-on jewels. Just peel off the gem and press it onto your drawing. Voilà! Now your zendoodle has some extra-special sparkle.

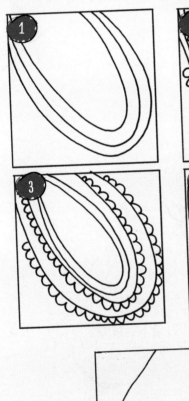

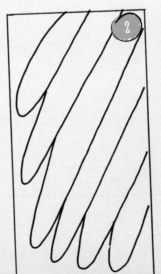

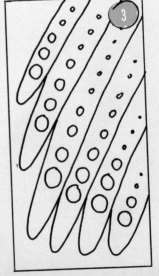

Mandala Elephant

Need a little calm in your day? Unwind as you embellish a noble elephant with a soothing, mandala-like design. Stack circles and craft symmetrical patterns for a unified look. Add a few petals, dots, and other decorations. You'll have a zendoodle that's pure bliss.

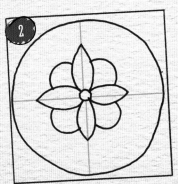

Making a Mandala

Construct a grid to keep your mandala balanced. Use a protractor to measure out even sections. Try 15 degrees to start. Then make layers using a compass. Place the needle in the center and draw circles with various diameters. Use your completed grid as a guide to creating symmetrical designs. Draw petals, triangles, and more in the sections, repeating them around the circle.

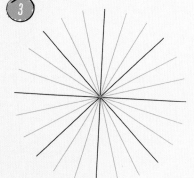

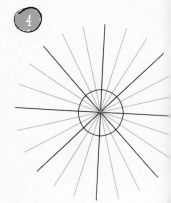

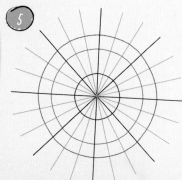

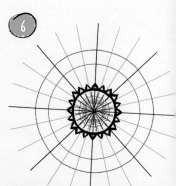

Get Crafty!

Zendoodles don't have to stay in your sketchbook. These fancy doodles are perfect for decorating and adding flair to everyday items. All you need is a little creativity. So if you're feeling artsy, try a variety of projects and crafts that'll showcase your zendoodles to the world. Be inspired to create your own DIY masterpiece — take your zendoodles off the page!

Zendoodle Rocks

Transform an ordinary rock into adorable artwork. Use permanent fine-tip markers for all your tiny details. Make a quirky owl by adding wide eyes, a little beak, and patterned wings. Try other animals or create rows of geometric designs. Be sure to use smooth, clean stones for effortless doodling.

One-of-a-kind Tote

Craft a handmade fashion statement! Fabric markers make it easy to take a white canvas bag from plain to extraordinary. Plan out your zendoodle in light pencil before using markers. Try using three-dimensional fabric paint to add fun textural accents.

Creative Cards

Brighten someone's day with a handcrafted note. Draw directly onto a blank card to add an easy personal touch. For a layered look, try cutting out your completed zendoodles. Mount the drawings onto colorful cardstock before gluing them onto the card. The cardstock will help the doodles stand out. Experiment with color, glitter, and other embellishments to make your card special.

Marble Magnets

Create bubbly zendoodle magnets for a satisfying afternoon craft. Start by tracing a flat glass marble onto thick paper. Doodle in the outline and cut it out. Brush decoupage glue onto the flat side of the marble. Press your paper circle onto it, with the zendoodle facing up. Add a layer of decoupage glue to the back of the paper. After it's dried, attach a magnet with a dab of hot glue. Make a matching set!

DIY Cell Phone Case

Show off your artsy side. Grab a white phone case and let your imagination do the rest. Be sure to use permanent markers for long-lasting doodles. If you like to change things up, pick up a clear phone case instead. Trace the case on paper. Draw your zendoodle inside the outline. Cut the paper out and slip it in the case. When you're ready for a new look, simply swap out the paper to showcase your latest design.

Original Origami

Add zendoodle flair to your favorite origami projects. Use abstract zendoodles to create custom origami paper. Simply draw on one side of the paper. See where your doodles peek out in the finished model. You can also decorate a completed model. Carefully place patterns and embellishments on the folded paper for an origami masterpiece.

Custom Keepsake Box

Store jewelry, trinkets, and more in style. Small wooden boxes and decoupage boxes are perfect blank canvases for pretty zendoodles. You can find the boxes at your local craft store. Use paint pens to draw your favorite animal with doodle accents. Or try decorating a plain brown box with white pen for a simple, but instantly elegant, look.

Can't wait to draw your own zendoodles?

Visit **capstonekids.com** to download blank outlines. Simply print and start doodling. Add your own unique curls, twirls, and tangles!

Read More

Ames, Lee J. *Draw 50 Animals: The Step-by-Step Way to Draw Elephants, Tigers, Dogs, Fish, Birds, and Many More....* Draw 50. New York: Watson-Guptill, 2012.

Corfee, Stephanie. *Quirky, Cute Doodles*. Doodle with Attitude. North Mankato, Minn.: Capstone Press, 2016.

Marbaix, Jane. *Zentangle for Kids*. New York: Sterling Children's Books, 2015.

Internet Sites

FactHound offers a safe, fun way to find Internet sites related to this book. All of the sites on FactHound have been researched by our staff.

Here's all you do:
Visit www.facthound.com
Type in this code: 9781515748403